ant

cm

1
2
3
4
5

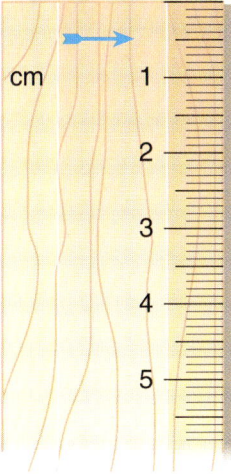

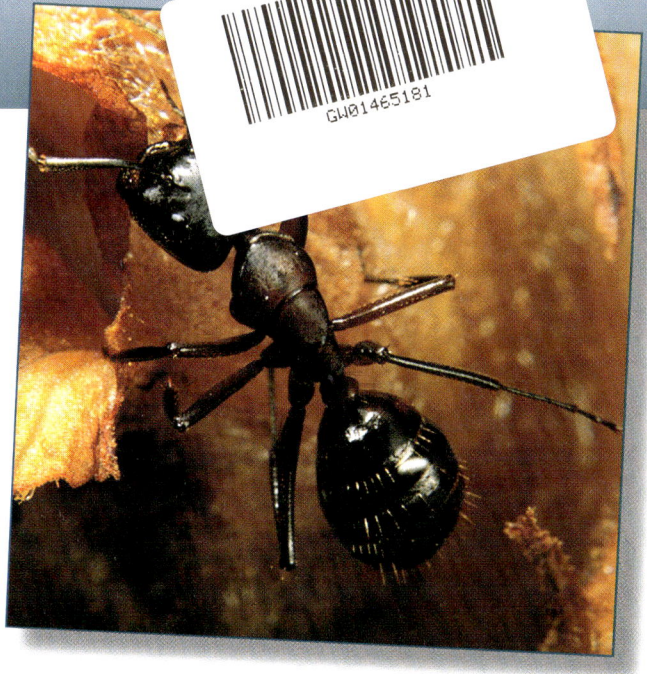

- found under stones and in lawns

- feeds on plants and other insects

- leaves a smell for other ants to follow

beetle

a
b
c
d
e
f
g
h
i
j
k
l
m
n
o
p
q
r
s
t
u
v
w
x
y
z

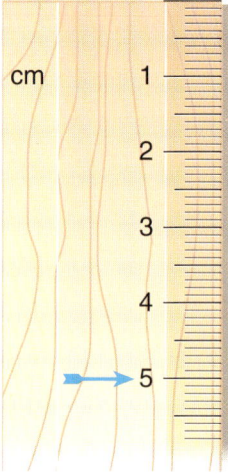
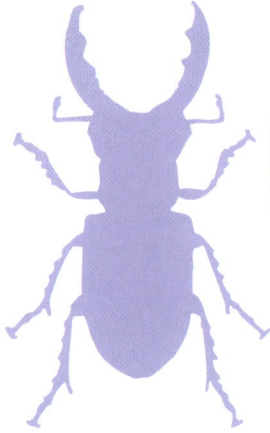

● found under logs and in dead leaves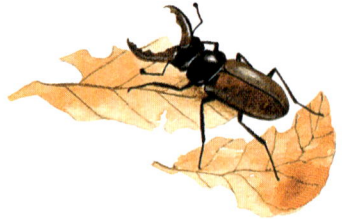

● feeds on dung and other insects

● can fly

butterfly

cm

6 5 4 3 2 1

a
b
c
d
e
f
g
h
i
j
k
l
m
n
o
p
q
r
s
t
u
v
w
x
y
z

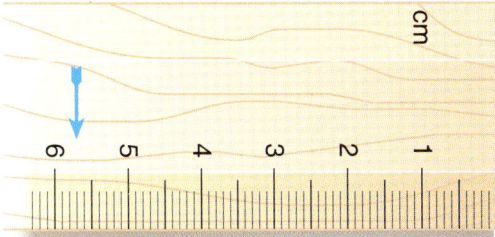

- found in gardens and hedgerows

- feeds on nectar

- starts its life as a caterpillar

3

centipede

a
b
c
d
e
f
g
h
i
j
k
l
m
n
o
p
q
r
s
t
u
v
w
x
y
z

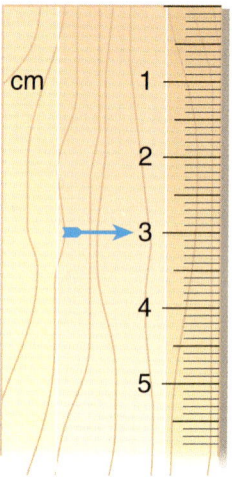

cm

1
2
3
4
5

- found under stones and dead leaves

- feeds on worms and slugs

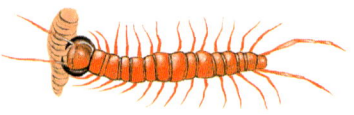

- some have more than 300 legs

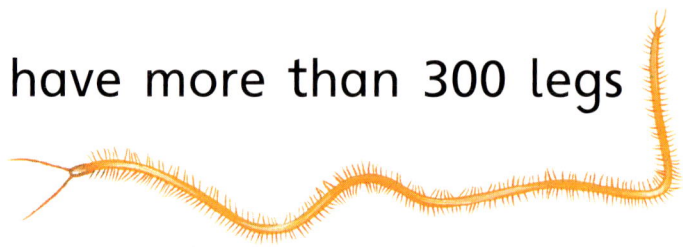

dragonfly

cm

1
2
3
4
5
6
7
8

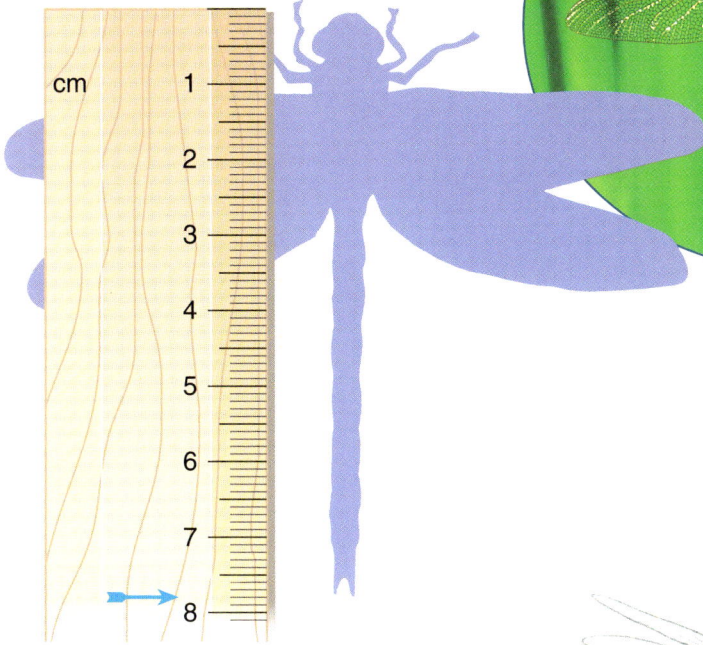

● found near
ponds and streams

● feeds on flying insects like
flies and beetles

● can fly very fast

grasshopper

a
b
c
d
e
f
g
h
i
j
k
l
m
n
o
p
q
r
s
t
u
v
w
x
y
z

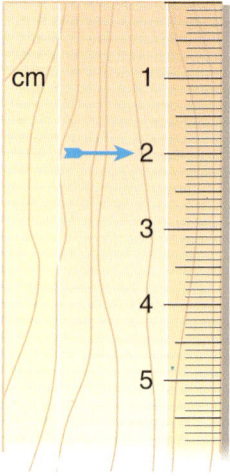

cm
1
2
3
4
5

- found in long grass and thick bushes

- feeds on grass and leaves

- makes a chirping sound with its back legs

honeybee

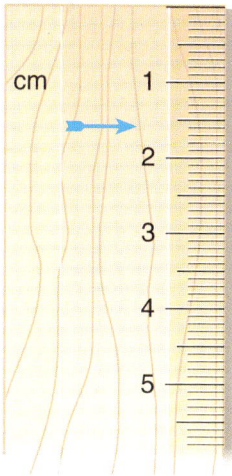

- **found on flowers and in hives**

- **feeds on nectar and pollen**

- **can sting if attacked**

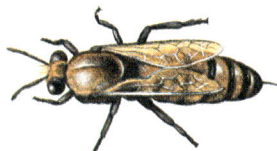

housefly

a
b
c
d
e
f
g
h
i
j
k
l
m
n
o
p
q
r
s
t
u
v
w
x
y
z

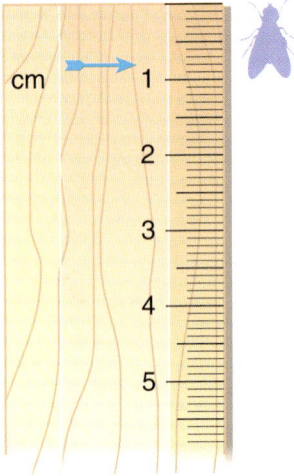

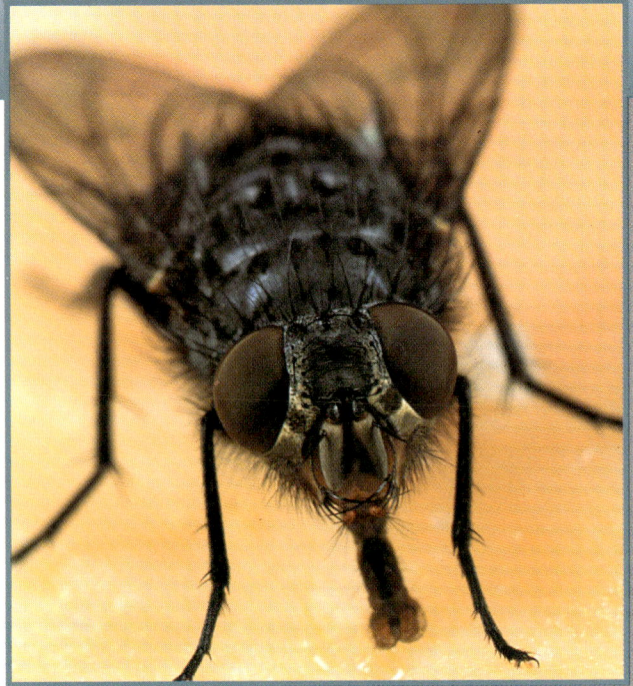

cm

1
2
3
4
5

● found in many habitats

● feeds on nectar and the juices of plants and animals

● makes a buzzing sound when it flies

ladybird

cm 1 2 3 4 5

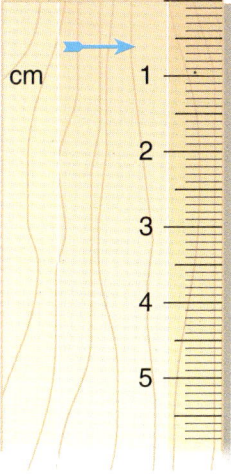

- found in parks and gardens

- feeds on small insects called aphids

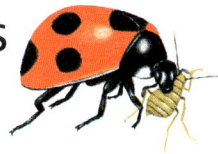

- can have from two to twenty four spots

millipede

a
b
c
d
e
f
g
h
i
j
k
l
m
n
o
p
q
r
s
t
u
v
w
x
y
z

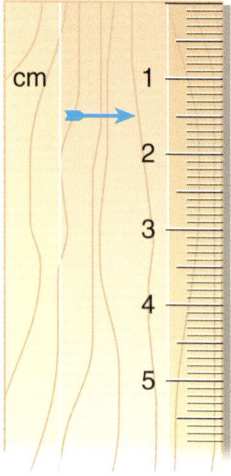

cm

1
2
3
4
5

- found under dead leaves

- feeds on rotting plants

- some can roll into a ball
  if frightened

mosquito

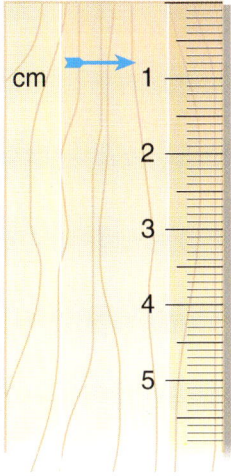

a
b
c
d
e
f
g
h
i
j
k
l
m
n
o
p
q
r
s
t
u
v
w
x
y
z

- found in many habitats

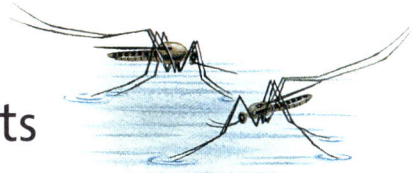

- male feeds on nectar, female feeds on blood

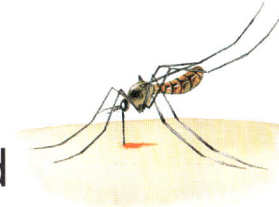

- some spread diseases

moth

a
b
c
d
e
f
g
h
i
j
k
l
m
n
o
p
q
r
s
t
u
v
w
x
y
z

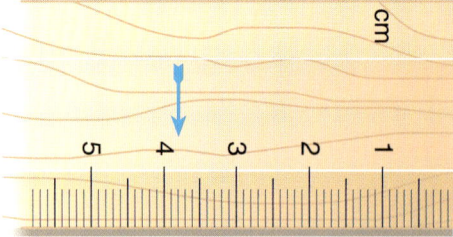

cm

5 4 3 2 1

- found in gardens and the countryside

- feeds on plants

- flies towards light

spider

1
2
3
4
5

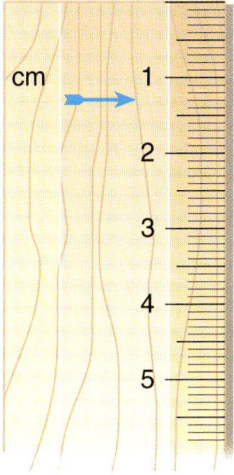

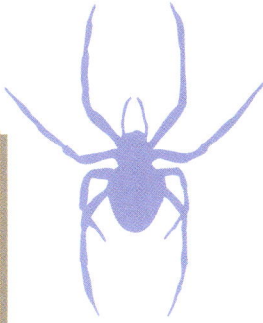

- found in many habitats

- feeds on insects which it catches in its web

- has up to eight eyes

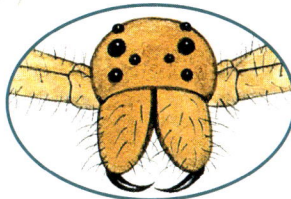

13

termite

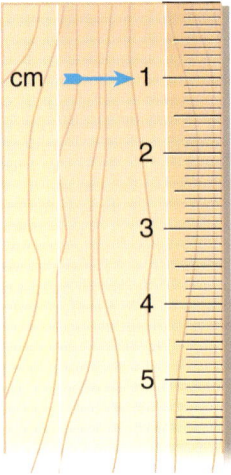

a
b
c
d
e
f
g
h
i
j
k
l
m
n
o
p
q
r
s
t
u
v
w
x
y
z

cm → 1
2
3
4
5

● found in many habitats

● feeds on wood and crops

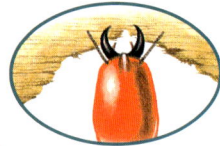

● some build huge nests

wasp

cm
1
2
3
4
5

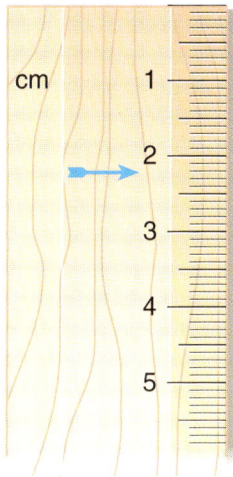

- found in gardens and parks

- feeds on fruit and sweet things

- can sting more than once if attacked

worm

cm

1
2
3
4
5
6
7
8
9
10
11
12
13
14
15

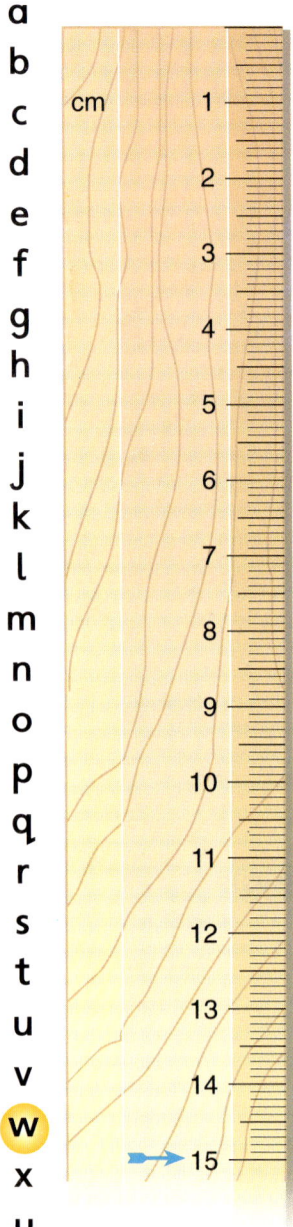

- found under the soil

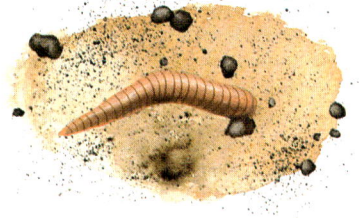

- feeds on dead leaves and soil

- one kind of worm can grow up to 30 metres long